The

Parish Churches

of

South West Essex

Drawn by

Charles ait

INTRODUCTION

This book covers the south west quarter of the county and consists of the Barnstable, Ongar, Chafford, Becontree, Havering and Waltham Hundreds. It also includes part of the Harlow Hundred which occurs geographically in the area to make up a comparatively numerical quarter of the county. As before I have described only the original parishes, leaving out all the more recent additions in large urban areas which may have more parish churches of later date. In fact there are so many that they merit an additional future volume to themselves. Also, because of boundary changes, much of Essex is now greater London, but because they were originally part of the county I have retained them as the Essex parishes they were when I started to draw and paint them years ago.

The Drawings

These are rendered into line drawings for printing purposes from the original watercolour paintings. Some of the more recent views record the changes which have taken place over the last forty to fifty years, especially in the cases where the buildings have ceased to be used as places of worship. This seems to be more frequent in this area of Essex than in other parts of the county. The locations of the buildings have changed with the construction of large housing and industrial centres which now surround them. As in previous books some alteration in foregrounds has been necessary in the interests of pictorial composition. In many cases, several sketches had to be made for each finished drawing.

Acknowledgements

To "Essex" by Nicholas Pevsner, "Essex" by G. Worley, "Essex Fonts and Font Covers" by W. Norman Paul, to my wife Joy, chauffeur, editor, etc., to typist Pauline Tracey and to the Royal Commission on Historical Monuments for the Hundreds listings.

This volume is dedicated to the memory of the late Peter James Came, himself a great Essex church lover and expert in local history.

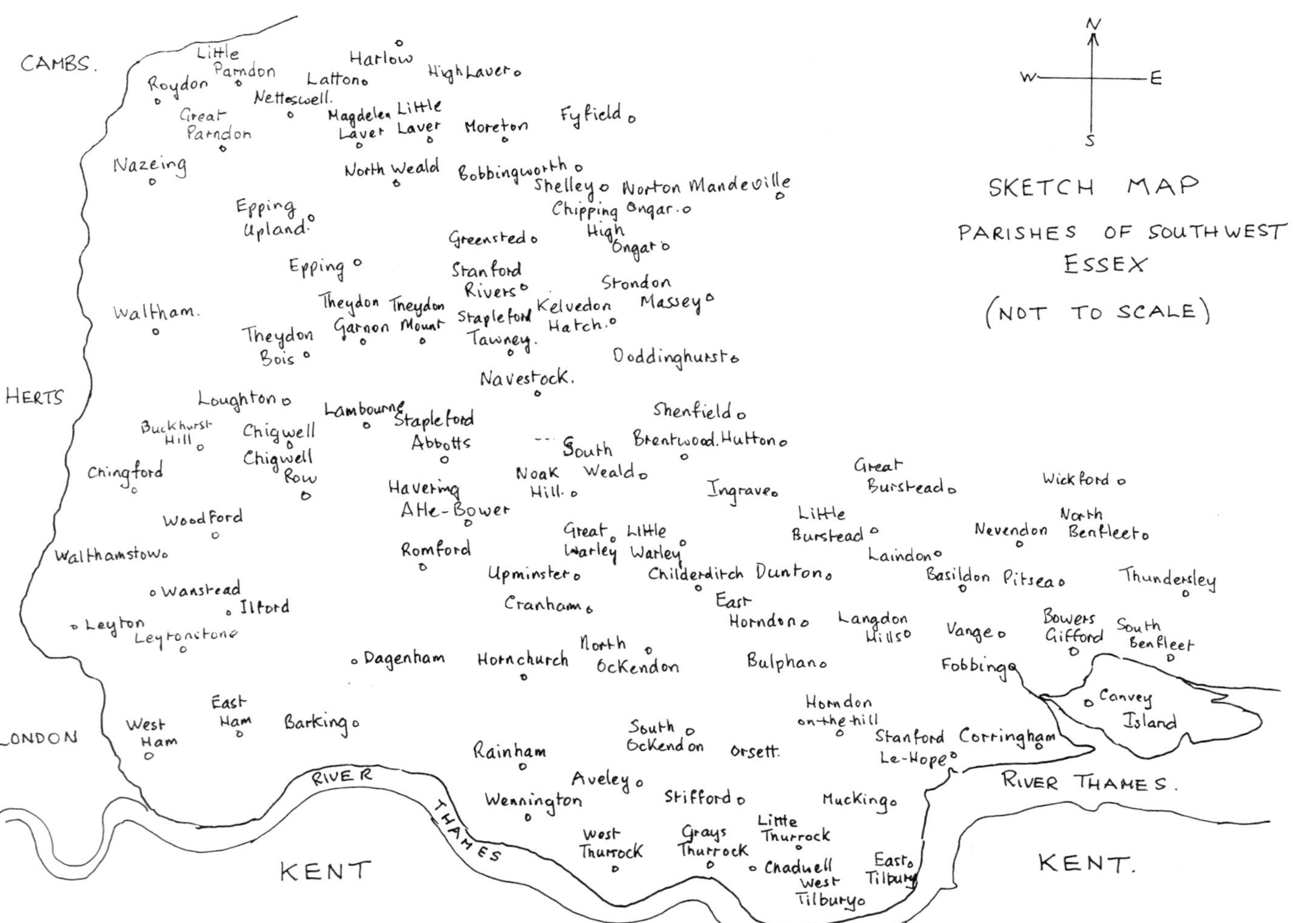
N
W
E
S
SKETCH MAP
PARISHES OF SOUTHWEST
ESSEX
(NOT TO SCALE)
CAMBS.
HERTS
LONDON
KENT
KENT.
RIVER THAMES
RIVER THAMES.
Little Parndon
Harlow
High Laver
Roydon
Latton
Netteswell.
Great Parndon
Magdelen Laver
Little Laver
Moreton
Fyfield
Nazeing
North Weald
Bobbingworth
Shelley
Norton Mandeville
Epping Upland.
Chipping Ongar.
High Ongar
Greensted
Epping
Stanford Rivers
Strondon Massey
Waltham.
Theydon Garnon
Theydon Mount
Stapleford Tawney.
Kelvedon Hatch.
Theydon Bois
Doddinghurst
Navestock.
Loughton
Lambourne
Stapleford Abbotts
Shenfield
Buckhurst Hill
Chigwell
Chigwell Row
South Weald
Brentwood.
Hutton
Chingford
Havering Atte-Bower
Noak Hill.
Ingrave
Great Burstead
Wickford
Little Burstead
North Benfleet
Nevendon
Woodford
Great Warley
Little Warley
Romford
Laindon
Walthamstow
Upminster
Childerditch
Dunton
Basildon
Pitsea
Thundersley
Wanstead
Ilford
Cranham
East Horndon
Langdon Hills
Vange
Bowers Gifford
South Benfleet
Leyton
Leytonstone
Dagenham
Hornchurch
North Ockendon
Bulphan
Fobbing
Canvey Island
East Ham
Horndon on-the-hill
West Ham
Barking
South Ockendon
Orsett.
Stanford Le-Hope
Corringham
Rainham
Aveley
Wennington
Stifford
Mucking
Little Thurrock
West Thurrock
Grays Thurrock
Chadwell
East Tilbury
West Tilbury

CONTENTS

Havering Hundred

	Page
Havering-atte-Bower – St. John the Evangelist	1
Hornchurch – St. Andrew	2
Noak Hill – St. Thomas	3
Romford – St. Edward the Confessor	4

Harlow Hundred

	Page
Great Parndon – St. Mary	5
Harlow – St. Mary and St. Hugh	6
Latton – St. Mary the Virgin	7
Little Parndon – St. Mary	8
Netteswell – St. Andrew	9
Potter Street – St. Mary Magdalen	10
Roydon – St. Peter	11

Waltham Hundred

	Page
Buckhurst Hill – St. John the Baptist	12
Chingford – All Saints	13
Chingford – St. Peter and St. Paul	14
Epping – St. John the Baptist	15
Epping Upland – All Saints	16
High Beech – Holy Innocents	17
Nazeing – All Saints	18
Upshire – St. Thomas	19
Waltham – Holy Cross	20

Becontree Hundred

	Page
Barking – St. Margaret	21
Dagenham – St. Peter and St. Paul	22
East Ham – St. Mary Magdalene	23
Great Ilford – St. Mary the Virgin	24
Little Ilford – St. Mary and St. Thomas of Canterbury	25
Leyton – St. Mary the Virgin	26
Leytonstone – St. John the Baptist	27
Walthamstow – St. Mary	28
Wanstead – St. Mary	29
West Ham – All Saints	30
Woodford – St. Mary the Virgin	31

Chafford Hundred

	Page
Aveley – St. Michael	32
Childerditch – All Saints	33
Cranham – All Saints	34
Grays Thurrock – St. Peter and St. Paul	35
Great Warley – St. Mary the Virgin	36
Little Thurrock – St. Mary the Virgin	37
Little Warley – St. Peter	38
North Ockendon – St. Mary Magdalen	39
Rainham – St. Helen and St. Giles	40
South Ockendon – St. Nicholas	41
South Weald – St. Peter	42
Stifford – St. Mary	43
Upminster – St. Laurence	44
Wennington – St. Mary and St. Peter	45
West Thurrock – St. Clement	46

Ongar Hundred

	Page
Abridge – Holy Trinity	47
Bobbingworth – St. Germain	48
Chigwell – St. Mary	49
Chigwell Row – All Saints	50
Chipping Ongar – St. Martin of Tours	51
Fyfield – St. Nicholas	52
Greensted-juxta-Ongar – St. Andrew	53
High Laver – All Saints	54
High Ongar – St. Mary	55
Kelvedon Hatch – St. Nicholas	56
Lambourne – St. Mary and All Saints	57
Little Laver – St. Mary the Virgin	58
Loughton – St. Nicholas	59
Loughton – St. John the Baptist	60
Loughton – St. Mary the Virgin	61
Magdalen Laver – St. Mary Magdalen	62
Moreton – St. Mary the Virgin	63
Navestock – St. Thomas the Apostle	64
North Weald Bassett – St. Andrew	65
Norton Mandeville – All Saints	66
Shelley – St. Peter	67
Stapleford Abbotts – St. Mary	68
Stapleford Tawney – St. Mary	69
Stanford Rivers – St. Margaret	70
Stondon Massey – St. Peter and St. Paul	71
Theydon Bois – St. Mary	72
Theydon Garnon – All Saints	73
Theydon Mount – St. Michael	74

Barstable Hundred

	Page
Basildon – Holy Cross	75
Billericay – St. Mary Magdalene	76
Bowers Gifford – St. Margaret	77
Brentwood – St. Thomas	78
Bulphan – St. Mary	79
Canvey Island – St. Katherine	80
Chadwell St. Mary – St. Mary	81
Corringham – St. Mary	82
Doddinghurst – All Saints	83
Downham – St. Margaret	84
Dunton – St. Mary	85
East Horndon – All Saints	86
East Tilbury – St. Catherine	87
Fobbing – St. Michael the Archangel	88
Great Burstead – St. Mary Magdalen	89
Horndon-on-the-Hill – St. Peter and St. Paul	90
Hutton – All Saints	91
Ingrave – St. Nicholas	92
Laindon – St. Nicholas	93
Langdon Hills (old) – St. Mary the Virgin and All Saints	94
Langdon Hills (new) – St. Mary	95
Little Burstead – St. Mary	96
Mucking – St. John the Baptist	97
Nevendon – St. Peter	98
North Benfleet – All Saints	99
Orsett – St. Giles and All Saints	100
Pitsea – St. Michael	101
Ramsden Bellhouse – St. Mary	102
Ramsden Crays – St. Mary	103
Shenfield – St. Mary the Virgin	104
South Benfleet – St. Mary	105
Stanford-le-Hope – St. Margaret of Antioch	106
Thundersley – St. Peter	107
Vange – All Saints	108
West Tilbury – St. James	109
Wickford – St. Catherine	110

CHARLES GRIGG TAIT
ST. JOHN THE EVANGELIST - HAVERING - ATTE - BOWER

Havering Hundred

Havering-atte-bower – St. John The Evangelist: Leave the A12 London to Chelmsford road turning left into the B175, proceeding north into the village and the church stands on the left of the road by a large village green complete with a stocks enclosure. A fairly large churchyard is entered through a brick capped stone wall. There are a few trees and shrubs and a small church hall in the churchyard. It is a Victorian building on an earlier site, built of flint in the Decorated style 1877, with a tower and six bells and an open passage under the tower. There is a Norman Purbeck marble font, 12th century. Registers date from 1670.

Hornchurch – St. Andrew: Leave Upminster and proceed due west into Hornchurch High Street. The very impressive tall church is on the left inside a large graveyard with many graves surrounded by a low wall and with a lych gate at the main entrance. There is a large complex built on to the south side to serve as a hall and offices. The church is a fine stone building of the 13th century with many 15th century additions and it was restored in 1869 and 1900. The embattled west tower has a tall spire with eight bells. Note the sculptured bull's head on the chancel end of the east window. There is some old stained glass, a sedilia and squint and several brasses. There are monuments to William Ayloffe 1517, Francis Rame 1617, Richard Blakestone 1638 and Richard Spencer 1784. Registers date from 1576.

Noak Hill – St. Thomas: Leave South Weald by Weald Road proceeding west through St. Vincents' Hamlet towards Havering-atte-Bower and turn right just after crossing the M25. The church is a short distance along a side road, standing on the right inside a small churchyard. It is entered by iron gates with several flagstone paths round the building. The area is surrounded by hedges and a few trees. The church is a red brick building with an octagonal turret, constructed in 1841-42. The parish was formed as a chapel of ease to Romford.

Romford – St. Edward The Confessor: The church stands on the north side of the market place behind a low stone wall inside a small churchyard. It is a fine tall structure, now rather dwarfed by the tall buildings of modern Romford. The building of Kentish ragstone was erected in 1850 on the site of an ancient chapel. The tower and spire, with eight bells, are prominent features. Several old monuments are retained including Sir Anthony Cooke 1576, Sir George Hervey and wife 1605 and Ann Carew 1605. Registers date from 1561.

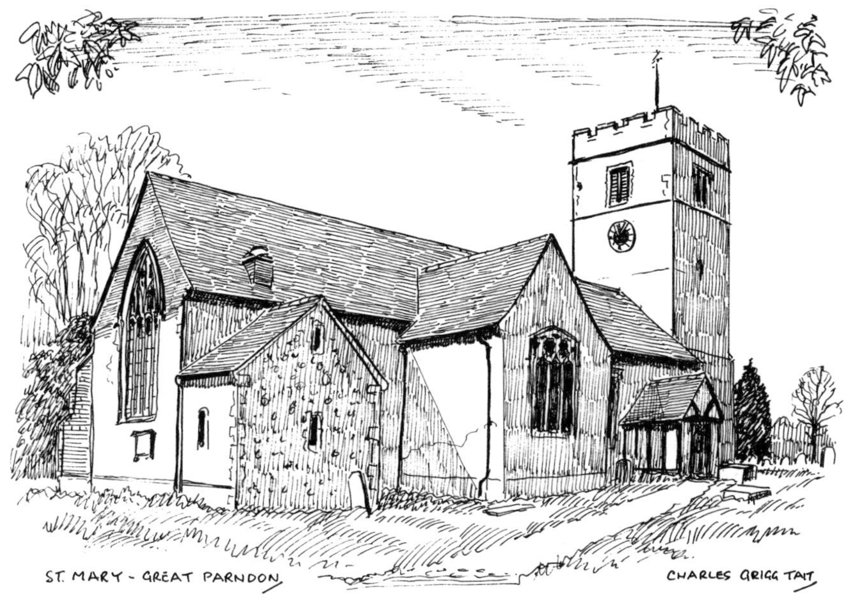

Harlow Hundred

Great Parndon – St. Mary: Proceed west along Edinburgh Way into Elizabeth Way, A1169. Turn left at the roundabout into Third Avenue and then sharp right at the roundabout into Peldon Road. The church stands on the left side inside a large very crowded graveyard surrounded by a wooden fence adjacent to a large car park. Of Perpendicular origin it is a stone structure with tower and four bells, all of the 15th century. There is a brass to Rowland Ramstone 1598 and some 15th century stained glass. The octagonal font is 15th century with some decorations on the faces and has a carved wooden cover. Registers date from 1547. Note:- A Premonstratension Abbey was founded here, but removed in 1180 to Beeleigh, near Maldon.

Harlow – St. Mary And St Hugh: From Chelmsford enter Harlow on the A414 turning right at the roundabout into Gildenway B183. Turn right again into Churchgate Street and the church is on the right of the road inside a medium sized churchyard surrounded by low iron railings and entered by a lych gate. The churchyard is neat and has stepping stones set into the turf. There are some trees and shrubs. The building is of Norman origin destroyed by fire in 1708 and rebuilt 1878-80 with a central tower and spire and with eight bells. The cruciform shape is unusual in Essex and the church retains 14th and 15th century features such as stained glass. There are many brasses in the north transept including a Knight and lady 1430, Robert Doncaster and wife 1490, Thomas Aylmer and wife 1518, Richard Bugges and wives 1636 and W. Newman and wife 1602. There are also monuments to Alexander Stafford and wife 1652 and John Wright 1659. Registers date from 1560.

Latton – St. Mary The Virgin: Proceed east along Second Avenue turning left at the roundabout into Howard Way and proceed north to join First Avenue, turning right at the sign First Avenue or Mandela Avenue. Turn left at Muskham Road and left again into the Gowers. The church stands back on the left behind a row of trees, inside a large churchyard. The building is of Norman origin, but mainly 16th century with an embattled west tower and four bells. There is much use of Roman bricks; the north chapel is 15th century. There is a table tomb and brass to Sir Peter Arderne and wife Katherine 1467 and brasses to William Harper and wife 1490, Frances Frankelin 1604, and James Altham and wife 1583. There are monuments to Sir Edward Altham 1632 and to Lady Campbell 1818. Registers date from 1560.

Little Parndon – St. Mary: Follow the A414 north towards Sawbridgeworth and turn left at the roundabout into Edinburgh Way. Proceed past Burnt Mill Warehouse area and turn right into Parndon Mill Lane. The church is on the left inside a small churchyard surrounded by a low brick and stone wall entered by wooden gates. The Rugby Club fields are adjacent to the churchyard and there is a car park. The church was completely rebuilt in 1868 with an apsidal end and small wooden tower. It was formerly one of the smallest parishes in the county.

Netteswell – St. Andrew: Follow Third Avenue east and at the roundabout join Second Avenue, A1025, turning right into Tripton Road and then left into Waterhouse Moor. The church stands inside a large uneven graveyard behind the Hummingbird public house. It is now the Harlow Study Centre. Of Norman/Saxon origin the church is a small stone building with a wooden south porch and belfry and three bells 1385 - 1418 and 13th and 15th century additions. On the outside wall of the chancel is an ornamental brickwork panel with the arms of Abbot Rase of Waltham 1497. There is some 15th century stained glass, a brass to Thomas Laurence and wife 1522 and to John Bannister and family 1607. Registers date from 1558.

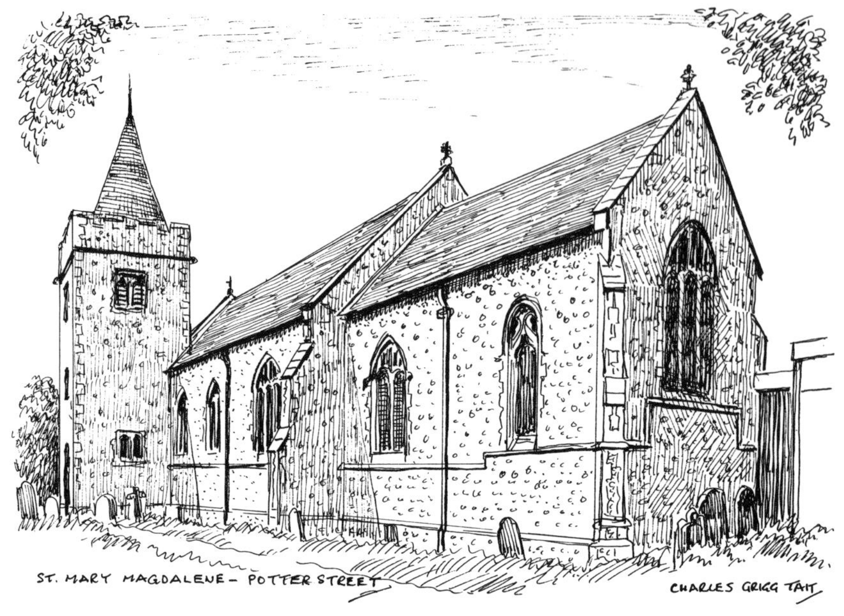

Potter Street – St. Mary Magdalene: Proceed along the A414 towards Chelmsford turning left into Potter Street at the signpost. Follow Potter Street and turn right into Church Road. The church is on the right side of the road inside a small churchyard behind a hedge and some trees. It is rather difficult to obtain a clear view as it is largely obscured by trees. The building is of medieval appearance, but was actually erected in 1831 with a small tower and shingled spire at a cost of £1,000.

Roydon – St. Peter: Follow the B181 north from Epping into the town and turn sharp left at the centre. The church stands on the left side inside a fairly large churchyard entered by a lych gate and surrounded by posts and chains. A number of trees prevent a clear view on the south side. Of Early English origin the church is a flint building of the 14th and 15th centuries, restored in 1854. There is a 14th century screen and the font is octagonal with some decoration, circa 1300. There are brasses to Thomas Colte and wife Joan, 1471, John Colte and two wives 1521, Elizabeth Stanley and five children 1589, a civilian 1580 and John Swifte 1570.

ST. JOHN THE BAPTIST – BUCKHURST HILL
CHARLES GRIGG TAIT

Waltham Hundred

Buckhurst Hill – St. John The Baptist: Leave Chingford by the A1009 going south east to join the B1393 going north towards Epping. Take the right junction signposted Loughton and Buckhurst Hill and the church is on the left of the road A121. Inside a large well laid out, but rather crowded graveyard, it is an imposing but new building. The present parish was formed out of Chigwell in 1838.

Chingford – All Saints: Leave Chingford Green going west on the A110 and then left at the police station into the Ridgeway. The church stands on the right side of the road high up in a small churchyard surrounded by a low brick wall. A few trees obscure the tower end and a new annexe has been added to the north side. The present building of ragstone was restored in 1929 after a long period of disuse and is mainly 13th century with a 16th century brick porch. Monuments are to Mary Leigh 1602, Sir Robert Leigh 1612 and Margaret Leigh 1624.

Chingford - St. Peter And St. Paul: Leave Waltham Abbey going south along the A112 and turn left at the junction with the A110 and the church is situated at the crossing by the traffic lights on the corner of Station Road and the Green. Inside a large, very crowded and uneven churchyard it is surrounded by a low brick wall topped by hedges and entered by several gates. The present building dates from 1844 and contains the square Purbeck marble font of the 12th century transitional Norman.

Epping – St. John The Baptist: The church stands in the centre of the town on the corner of the High Street and St. John's road. It is a large tall impressive building with a clock tower. It was erected in 1832 and rebuilt in 1890. The tower was erected in 1908. The new parish was created in 1889 and the new church built in 14th century style.

Epping Upland – All Saints: Leave the road from Epping going south west and turn off right along the B182. The church stands on a sharp corner on the left side of the road inside a large churchyard behind a wooden fence entered by two sets of wooden gates. A number of tall trees obscure the tower end. The church is of Norman origin and later, but was largely restored in 1878. The embattled west tower is 16th century and the square font is 13th century Early English. Registers date from 1539.

High Beech - Holy Innocents: Take the A112 south–from Waltham Abbey and take any of the left turns into the forest. The church stands inside a large churchyard surrounded by a low stone wall and entered by a small lych gate. It is in the centre of a forest area and the approach roads all have traffic calming measures to restrict speeds. Owing to the tall trees a clear view of the church is rather difficult to obtain. The parish was formed out of Waltham Abbey in 1837 and the new church was built in 1873. Registers date from 1839.

Nazeing – All Saints: Leave Epping Upland and proceed along the B181 to Broadley Common, turning sharp left and then right through the village to a sign 'Church Only' into a car park. The church stands on the left at the end of a gravel path passing through a lych gate. Many trees obscure the church and the churchyard. Of Norman origin, the church is built of flint and rubble of 13th century with a 15th century brick tower. The south porch is 15th century timber. There was considerable restoration in 1871 and 1894. The octagonal font with some decoration is 15th century Perpendicular. The rood loft staircase is in good condition. Registers date from 1559.

Upshire – St. Thomas: Leave the B1393 road going south from Epping at the sign Upshire and the church is situated on the left side of the road approaching Waltham Abbey. Inside a medium sized, rather uneven churchyard, it is surrounded by hedges and entered by a small lych gate. The approach to the church is by a gravel path and a line of yew trees. It was built in 1902.

Waltham Abbey – Holy Cross And St. Laurence: The imposing remains of the great abbey stand in the centre of the town in large and extensive grounds, surrounded by stone and brick walls. The area is very well laid out with detailed diagrams at strategic points for the benefit of the visitor. The approaches to the church are by flagstone paths on all sides. The building is of Norman foundation on a Saxon site and contains much Norman architecture inside with later additions of the 13th and 14th century, too numerous to include in a short description. Originally a priory it was dissolved in 1540. The octagonal font is 12th century Purbeck marble and there are brasses to various people of 1555, 1576 and 1599. Some extensive restoration took place in 1859-60. Registers date from 1663.

Becontree Hundred

Barking – St. Margaret: From East Ham proceed east along the A13, turning off left at the sign Barking. The church is situated in the grounds of the old abbey and the main entrance is through the abbey gateway, the Curfew Tower. The graveyard is quite open and well laid out with many pathways. The church has been much enlarged recently with additional buildings to the south side. Of Norman origin, it is an imposing building of Kentish ragstone with a tall embattled west tower of mainly 15th century work with some Norman traces and with eight bells. There are brasses to a priest 1450, Thomas Broke and wife 1493, John Tedcastell and wife 1596, Richard Halet 1485 and monuments to Martin, the first vicar, Sir Charles Montague 1625, Francis Fuller 1636, John Bennett 1706 and Sir Orlando Humphreys 1737. The font is 16th century. Registers date from 1558. Note:- Captain James Cook was married here in 1762 to Elizabeth Batts.

Dagenham – St. Peter And St. Paul: Leave Romford and proceed south past Oldchurch hospital, towards the dock area and signposted Rainham, turning right, at the junction with the A125. Immediately past the crossroads with the A112 and the B178 turn right into Church Lane and the church stands on the right inside a large open and uneven graveyard with many stones. It is opposite the Cross Keys public house and inside a low brick wall with iron gates and opposite the church carpark. The building is mainly 13th century, but largely rebuilt in 1800 and 1878 retaining much of the old materials including the Tudor north chapel. Note the rather unusual carved battlements on the tower and nave. There are monuments to Sir Thomas Urswyck and wife 1479 and to Sir Richard Alibon 1688. Registers date from 1546.

East Ham – St. Mary Magdalene: From Ilford proceed west along the A118 turning left into the A117 and south into East Ham. The church stands on the left at the junction of High Street South and the A13. Inside a large crowded graveyard, uneven in places, with many trees it is surrounded by a brick wall entered by iron gates. The apsidal end is rather obscured and difficult to view properly. The church is of Norman origin, built of flint with an embattled west tower and apsidal chancel with 13th century additions. There is use of Roman bricks, Tudor woodwork and a Norman painting in the chancel. Monuments include brasses to Hester Neve 1610, Elizabeth Heigham 1622, Edward Nevill 17th century, William Heigham and wife 1620, Giles Breame 1610 and Higham Beamish 1723. The font is 17th century. Registers date from 1696.

ST. MARY THE VIRGIN – GREAT ILFORD
CHARLES GRIGG TAIT

Great Ilford – St. Mary The Virgin: From Romford proceed west along the A118 or Romford road and after passing Seven Kings station the church stands on the left at the junction with Buckingham Road. Inside a very large graveyard and adjacent to the cemetery it is surrounded by a brick wall and iron railings with many entrances through iron gates. It is a very large building and was erected in 1831 to serve as the parish church. It has twice been enlarged. There are several other parish churches in the urban area.

ST. MARY THE VIRGIN – GREAT ILFORD
CHARLES GRIGG TAIT

Little Ilford – St. Mary And St. Thomas Of Canterbury: Proceed west from Great Ilford church along the A118 turning right into Little Ilford Lane and then right into Church Road. The church is situated on the left on the corner of St. Winifriede's Avenue inside a medium sized churchyard surrounded by a black stone wall entered by metal gates. It is very neatly kept with some tall trees and shrubs. The building is of Norman origins with much modernisation. The chancel was rebuilt of brick in 1724 as was the south porch. There are monuments to John Lethieullier 1737, Smart Lethieullier and wife 1760, Thomas Heron 1517, William 1614 and Ann 1630 Hyde and William Waldegrave, wife and family 1610. Registers date from 1539.

ST. MARY THE VIRGIN – LEYTON
CHARLES GRIGG TAIT

Leyton – St. Mary And St. Edward: From Leytonstone Church proceed along Church Lane, following a rather meandering route into Grove Green and then turn right into Leyton High Road. Proceed north along the High Road and turn left into Church Road. The church stands on the right side of the road opposite a pub 'The Two Finches' and a Cash and Carry Beauty Depot; inside a very large and crowded graveyard behind iron railings and a brick wall. It is entered by iron gates and is surrounded by many trees. The building was erected in 1832, having an earlier red brick tower of 1659 and an 18th century clock turret. More additions were made in 1889 and 1932. Monuments include Ursula Gasper 1493, Sir Michael Hicks and wife 1612, Sir William Hicks 1680 and son; William 1703, John Storey 1787, William Bosanquet 1813 and many others of later date. Registers date from 1575.

ST. MARY THE VIRGIN – LEYTON
AND ST. EDWARD.
CHARLES GRIGG TAIT

Leytonstone – St. John The Baptist: From Eastern Avenue, proceed west along Cambridge Park Road and turn left at the junction into Leytonstone High Road. The church stands on the right at the junction with Church Lane inside a medium sized churchyard surrounded by a high brick wall topped by iron railings. It is entered by iron gates and tall brick pillars. There are many trees and shrubs which tend to obscure a clear view. The building, erected in 1832, is in the early English style, of bricks, with additions in 1893 and 1902 and it has a small west tower.

Walthamstow – St. Mary And St. Stephen: From Walthamstow Central Station proceed north along Hoe Street turning right into Church Hill Road and again into Church End. The church is at the end of a cul-de-sac opposite the Monoux Alms Houses, inside a very large churchyard with many tombs and gravestones, surrounded by iron railings leading into Church Lane. It is a brick building with an embattled west tower and ten bells. It was rebuilt in 1535 by Sir George Monoux and enlarged in 1818, 1843 and 1876. There are monuments to Sir George Monoux and wife 1543, Lady Lucy Stanley 1630, Sir Thomas and Lady Merry 1633, Sigismund Trafford and family 1723, Bonell family 1690 and Elizabeth Morley 1637. Registers date from 1645.

Wanstead – St. Mary: From Gallow's Corner proceed westward along Eastern Avenue into Wanstead. Turn left into Blake Hall Road and left again in Overton Drive. The church is on the right of the road inside a very large churchyard behind tall iron gates surrounded by many trees and shrubs, making a clear view difficult. It has a very impressive entrance with tall pillars and steps. A large brick and stone building it was rebuilt on the site of an older building in 1790 in classical style. Inside are high box pews and a pulpit with sounding board. There are monuments to Sir Josiah Child and son 1699 and George Bowles 1817. Registers dates from 1640.

West Ham – All Saints: Continue along the A118 turning left into Green Street and then right into Plaistow New Road and turning right into Church Street. The church stands on the right inside a large, open, grassy churchyard with very few gravestones and approached by several iron gates. The main entrance from the road is by a long covered lych gate. It is quite a large impressive church. The building is of Norman origin, but mainly built of brick and stone, 15th century, with tall embattled west tower and ten bells. It was much restored in the 19th century. There are monuments to Thomas Staples 1592, John Faldo 1613, Francis Faldo 1632, William Fawcit and wife 1631, Thomas Foot 1688, Nicholas Buckeridge and wife 1638 and James Cooper and wife 1743. On the outside south wall is a sundial 1803. Registers date from 1653.

Woodford – St. Mary The Virgin: From Walthamstow proceed north along the A104 into Woodford, turning right into Woodford Green High Road. The church stands on the right side just past the junction with Chelmsford Road, inside a large open churchyard with many graves and paths. It has an impressive entrance from the road with a flight of steps up to the doorway. The building is red brick of 1817, with a west tower 1708, restored in 1889, and is very large. There are monuments to Rowland Elvington and wife 1595 and Charles Foulis 1783. Registers date from 1638.

Chafford Hundred

Aveley – St. Michael: Leave Stifford towards South Ockendon along the B186, turning left into the B1335 and the church stands on the left side of the road inside a large crowded churchyard surrounded by brick walls and hedges and entered through a large stone arch and iron gates. A flagstone path leads up to the north porch. Of Norman origin, the building has much original Norman and Early English work, but was largely restored in 1886. The west tower is 13th century and the rood screen is 15th century. The square Norman font with some decorations is of Purbeck marble of the 12th century. There are brasses to Ralph de Knevynton 1370, Elizabeth Bacon 1583 and Bacon children 1588. Registers date from 1563.

Childerditch – All Saints And St. Faith's: Proceed towards Southend on the A127 and about halfway between the M25 and the East Horndon Halfway House, turn left into Childerditch Lane. The church stands high up on a hill overlooking a fishing lake. It is approached along a narrow track. The churchyard which is quite large, but very uneven, is entered through an open gateway set in surrounding hedges. It is a rather remote little church overlooking the Thames. The small building is constructed of Kentish ragstone, rebuilt in 1869 on the site of a previous church. There is an old lectern and the octagonal font is 16th century Tudor. Registers date from 1537.

Cranham – All Saints: Leave the A127 from Southend just before approaching the M25, turning left at Warley Hall Lane and right after crossing the railway bridge. Proceed west passing under the M25 into Cranham village. Turn left immediately after the railway bridge, along a narrow road, and the church stands inside a large churchyard, entered by open gates through a brick wall. Although the churchyard is rather uneven there are flagstone paths all round. There is a small church hall nearby. The old church was pulled down and the new stone building was rebuilt in 1874 in Early English style, retaining some parts of the original church. It is a fine, tall and imposing building. There is a monument to Major General James Edward Oglethorpe 1698 - 1785, the founder of the British colony of Georgia, who lived for a time at Cranham Hall. Registers date from 1558.

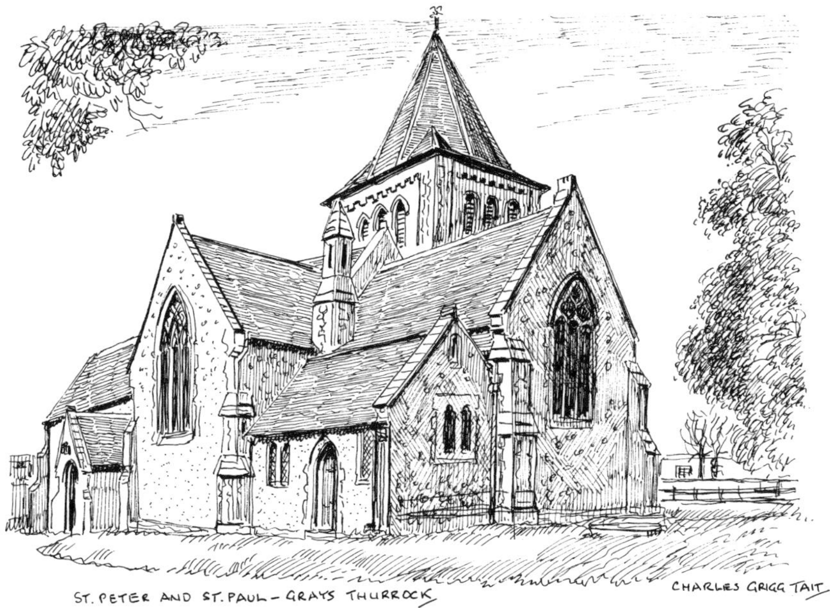

ST. PETER AND ST. PAUL – GRAYS THURROCK CHARLES GRIGG TAIT

Grays Thurrock – St. Peter And St. Paul: Leave the A13 westwards from Stanford-le-Hope turning south either by the A1013 or the A1012 and the church is situated south of the railway at the end of the High Street, quite near to the railway station. It is on the right side of the road inside a medium sized churchyard surrounded by brick walls and iron railings. A large flint building, the church is of 13th century origin, but almost entirely rebuilt in 1846. Some portions of the old church are retained inside the chancel, The octagonal font is 15th century Perpendicular and there are brasses to a woman and family 1510. Registers date from 1674.

ST. PETER AND ST PAUL – GRAYS THURROCK CHARLES GRIGG TAIT

Great Warley – St. Mary The Virgin: Leave Brentwood going south into Great Warley and proceed along the B186 turning left at the Thatchers Arms into Great Warley Street. The church stands on the right inside a large churchyard entered by a lych gate. Several tall trees rather obscure the building. The old church of St. Peter was replaced by the new church of brick erected in 1904. The interior is particularly noted for the elaborate decoration in aluminium and bronze in the chancel. Registers date from 1539.

ST. MARY THE VIRGIN – GREAT WARLEY
CHARLES GRIGG TAIT

ST. MARY THE VIRGIN- LITTLE THURROCK
CHARLES GRIGG TAIT

Little Thurrock (East Thurrock) – St. Mary The Virgin: Leave Chadwell St. Mary and proceed westwards towards Grays Thurrock, crossing the A1089 into a built up area. The church is situated on the left side of the road inside a small churchyard surrounded on all sides by brick walls. The approach to the north porch is by a gravel path. The building shows traces of Norman origins, but is mainly 13th century and heavily restored in 1878-9 in the 14th century style. Some earlier features have been retained. Registers date from 1654.

ST. MARY THE VIRGIN – LITTLE THURROCK
CHARLES GRIGG TAIT

Little Warley – St. Peter: Turn left off the A127 from Southend between the East Horndon Halfway House and the M25. The church stands immediately on the right inside a small uneven churchyard entered by wooden gates. It is a small stone building of 16th century on an earlier site. A red brick tower was added in 1718. The timber south porch is circa 1500. There is a brass to Anne Hamer 1592, Sir Denner Strutt and wife 1641 and to Lady Strutt 1658. The octagonal font is 18th century. Registers date from 1539.

North Ockendon – St. Mary Magdalene: Leave the A127 from Southend just before the M25 and turn left into the B186, turning off right, then left, into a narrow road Church Lane, past a sportsfield. The church stands inside a small churchyard approached by a gravel path and an avenue of tall trees surrounded by farm buildings. Rather a fine impressive building of Norman origin, the church is built of flint, with an embattled west tower and five bells. It was restored in 1858 and again in recent times. The building shows a wide variety of periods and styles. The chapel is named after the Poyntz family and contains several marble tombs, including Sir Gabriel and Lady Poyntz. There are brasses to William Poyntz and family 1502, to John Poyntz 1547, to Thomasine Badby and to Thomas Poyntz 1709. There is some stained heraldic glass of the 13th century. Registers date from 1570.

Rainham – St. Helen And St. Giles: Leave Wennington and continue westward along the B1335 into Rainham and the church stands on the right on a sharp corner inside a neat triangular church-yard surrounded by a wall and entered by iron gates. This corner is very busy with road traffic. The church is an almost complete example of late Norman work even to the west tower. Some additions have been made, but the Norman church has been carefully preserved. The circular font is of Saxon-Norman origin of the 12th century and there are many Norman windows. There is a brass to a civilian 1500 and to a lady 1480. Registers date from 1665.

South Ockendon – St. Nicholas: Proceed south from the A127 along the B186 and the church stands on the left just before entering the village. Inside a large churchyard it is entered by wooden gates through a stone wall. Opposite the churchyard is a picturesque green crossed by roads and adjacent to the Royal Oak public house. Of Norman origin the church has a circular tower with battlements of the 13th century. The fabric is mainly 13th century with some Norman work. The timber porch is 15th century. There is a brass to Sir Ingelram Bruyn 1400, to Margaret Bake 1602 and to Sir Richard Salton-Stall, Lord Mayor of London 1601.

South Weald – St. Peter: Leave the Brentwood High Street A1023 turning right into Wigley Bush Road and proceed north into South Weald. The church stands impressive at the crossroads inside a large churchyard entered by a lych gate through a stone wall. There is a large church car park at the eastern end. A few trees tend to obscure the tower end. Of Norman origin the church is a massive, tall building, mainly 15th century, but restored in 1868. The embattled west tower is of Kentish ragstone with six bells and a turret. There is some Norman work in the walls. The timber south porch is restored 15th century work. There is some early stained glass and several small brasses of various dates from 1450. The octagonal font is 1662. Registers date from 1540.

Stifford – St. Mary: Leave Orsett village continuing westward about three miles and the church is on the left side of the road, inside a large rather crowded graveyard, which is entered by iron gates in a stone wall. The road is very narrow here. The church is built of flint and stone of 13th century origin with a 13th century tower and spire and was thoroughly restored in 1862. There is a monument to David de Tillebery 1330 and six brasses to Ralph Perche 1375, John Ardalle and wife 1504, to William Lathom and wife 1622, Ann Lathom 1627 and Elizabeth Lathom 1630 and there are some 16th and 17th century monuments. The square font is early 13th century. Registers date from 1568.

Upminster – St. Lawrence: Leave the A127 from Southend at the Chapman's Farm junction and proceed south. After passing Upminster station turn sharp right into St. Mary's Lane and the church is on the left inside a large churchyard behind a low brick wall, entered by iron gates and other entrances. There are many trees that tend to obscure the building. A new annexe has been built on the south side. The building is of Norman origin, but mainly 13th century. The rubble built west tower has a timber belfry and octagonal spire. Restoration took place in 1862, but much of the early church was retained. There are brasses to Roger Deincourt and wife 1455, Nicholas Wayte and wife 1542, Andrew Branfill 1709 and James Esdaille 1812. Registers date from 1543.

Wennington – St. Mary And St. Peter: From Aveley continue westward along the B1335 crossing the A13 towards Rainham and the church is situated on the left side of the road which is very narrow here. It stands inside a small uneven graveyard entered by iron gates in a low stone wall. The building is of Norman foundation, of stone with Kentish ragstone, and an embattled west tower of later date. Some restoration took place in 1866 and other alterations have occurred at various times. The octagonal font of Purbeck marble is 13th century and there is a mural tablet to Henry Bust 1624. Registers date from 1757.

ST. MARY AND ST PETER – WENNINGTON
CHARLES GRIGG TAIT

West Thurrock – St. Clement: Leave Grays Thurrock proceeding westward along the A126 into West Thurrock. The church is hidden amongst a mass of tall industrial buildings and can be approached by road or better by a footpath opposite the Ship public house. Proceed south by the St. Clement Hall and cross the railway line into West Thurrock road. The church stands on the left inside a small churchyard, which is now designated as a wild life conservation area. The firm of Proctor and Gamble have donated a large sum of money towards maintaining both the church fabric and preserving the graveyard. The church is of 13th century origin with some 14th century additions and the west tower is 1450 with a brick top. The octagonal font with some decoration is Perpendicular. There are brasses to Humphrey Heies and son 1584 and to Sir Christopher Helford and Lady Helford 1608. Registers date from 1681.

Ongar Hundred

Abridge – Holy Trinity: Proceed along the A113 into the village and the church is a small building on the left facing directly onto the road. There is no space for a churchyard and the church can very easily be missed because of its position between other buildings. It is a small brick building erected as a chapel of ease to Lambourne in 1833 and enlarged in 1877.

Bobbingworth – St. Germain: The church stands on the left side of the road leading off the A122, behind a fenced-in green inside a fairly crowded churchyard. With a well trimmed hedge in front it is entered by two sets of wooden gates. Several large trees line the south side and make it difficult to obtain a clear view. The building is of Early English origin, largely restored in 1841 and with 19th century additions. The west tower of white brick contains the porch. The pulpit is 17th century and there are some 17th century monuments and brasses. The octagonal Perpendicular font is 15th century. Registers date from 1558.

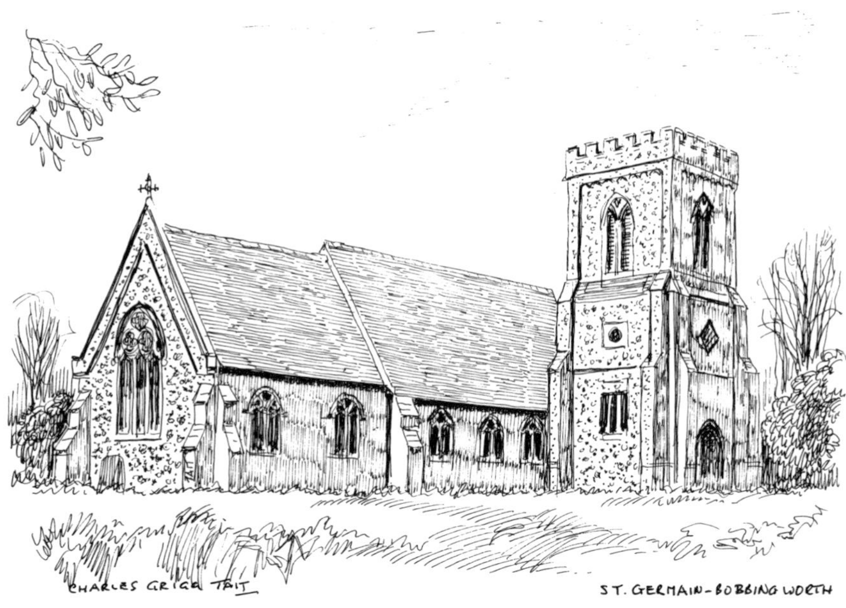

Chigwell – St. Mary: Proceed along the A113 into the village and opposite the Kings Head Inn the church stands on a corner with Roding Lane. It is inside a very large churchyard bordered on the road side by a brick wall and entered by two sets of gates and by hedges and other entrances on the other sides. The church is of Norman origin, but much restored in 1888. There is some Norman work retained and much 15th century as well. The belfry is white weather board with a spire and there is a timber south porch. There is a brass to Samuel Harsnett, vicar and later Archbishop of York 1631, in full ecclesiastic vestments. Registers date from 1555.

Chigwell Row – All Saints: Leave the A12 London to Chelmsford road, turning left into the A1112 and proceed north. The church stands prominently on the right side of the dual carriageway close to the crossroads. Inside a medium sized churchyard it is entered by two gates, one a lych gate, behind a stone wall and adjacent to the church car park. The church is largely obscured by many trees and shrubs and it is difficult to obtain a clear view. It is a fine large building with a tall embattled tower and an impressive entrance. Constructed of yellow stone with white dressings, it was erected in 1867 in 13th century style.

CHARLES GRIGG TAIT
ST. MARTIN OF TOURS – CHIPPING ONGAR.

Chipping Ongar – St. Martin Of Tours: Follow the A128 from Brentwood into the town and the church stands on the right side of the main street inside a small churchyard, surrounded by iron railings and buildings which rather overcrowd it. The church is of Norman origin with many early Norman traces and Roman tiles. The timber belfry is 15th century and there is some Tudor brickwork in a window. There was some restoration in 1884 and 1887. The square font is 14th century. Registers date from 1538.

ST. MARTIN OF TOURS – CHIPPING ONGAR
CHARLES GRIGG TAIT

Fyfield – St. Nicholas: On entering the village, leave the B184 at the church sign. The church stands on the right side of the road inside a large cleared churchyard, bordered on all sides by a low hedge and entered by a brick and iron gateway. A line of pollarded trees lines the road side. The building is of Norman origin with much Roman brick in the fabric. It consists of chancel, nave with aisles and central tower rebuilt in the 19th century. Mostly of 13th and 14th century construction it was restored in 1853 and 1893. The square Norman font of the 12th century has some decorated faces. Registers date from 1538.

Greensted-juxta-Ongar – St. Andrew: Leave Chipping Ongar going south along the A128, turn right at the sign Greensted Church and proceed along a narrow road to another sign Greensted Church. The church stands on the right side of the road, inside a small churchyard, surrounded by hedges and entered through wooden gates. This famous little building is considered to be the oldest wooden church in the world with timber walls of Saxon split oak logs, extensively repaired in the 19th century so that the logs are now only four feet long. Tradition has it that St. Edmund's body rested here one night on its way from London to Bury St. Edmunds. The church has been added to in Tudor times and later. Registers date from 1561.

High Laver – All Saints: The church stands on the left side of the road, just after the crossroads going south towards Moreton and the A122. Inside a fairly large well kept churchyard it is bordered on the road side by an elaborate iron fence on a brick wall and entered by an iron gate of similar design. The building is of Norman origin with Roman bricks in the fabric and later 13th and 14th century additions. The west tower is 14th century with 18th century brickwork added with battlements and spire. The church was restored in 1865. Monuments include a brass to Edward Sulyard and wife Myrabyll 1500 and a tablet with an inscription commemorates the grave of John Locke, the philosopher 1704. The octagonal Perpendicular font, 15th century, has some decorated faces. Registers date from 1553.

High Ongar – St. Mary: The church stands on the left side of the road going west from Chipping Ongar through the village, which is now by-passed away from the A122. It stands behind a low brick wall inside a fairly large and well spread out churchyard, a line of trees screening the building from the main road. Of Norman origin with nave and chancel it has a brick tower added in 1858. The south doorway is very impressive with elaborate decoration and is a chief feature of the church. There was some restoration in 1884, but the 17th century pulpit and some poppy head bench ends were preserved. There is a monument to a civilian 1510. Registers date from 1538.

Kelvedon Hatch – St. Nicholas: At the crossroads in Brentwood, opposite Wilson's corner, turn into the Ongar road A128 and proceed north. The church stands on the right side of Church Road inside a large churchyard surrounded by trees and hedges, entered through two sets of wooden gates. The church was twice rebuilt, in 1740 and again in 1895, of brick in the 13th century style. There are several 17th century monuments and brasses. Registers date from 1561.

Lambourne – St. Mary And All Saints: From Stapleford Abbotts proceed north and turn left into the A113 towards Abridge. Before entering the village turn left into a long narrow road which ends at Lambourne Hall. The church stands on the left side of the road behind a low white fence entered through a white gate and a kissing gate. The churchyard is large and open with a few trees and many gravestones. The church is a small stone building of Norman origin with a wooden bell tower, remodelled in the early Georgian period. The north and south doorways are Norman as are some windows. There is some 17th century stained glass and a brass to Robert Barfott and wife, 1546, and children and several monuments to the Lockwood family. The hexagonal font is 18th century. Registers date from 1583.

ST. MARY AND ALL SAINTS – LAMBOURNE
CHARLES GRIGG TAIT

ST. MARY THE VIRGIN - LITTLE LAVER
CHARLES GRIGG TAIT

Little Laver – St. Mary The Virgin: The small church stands on the right side of the road from Fyfield to Matching, inside a small well kept churchyard surrounded by a hedge with an unusual holly bush trimmed in the shape of a cross. The building is of Norman origin with an apsidal end to the chancel and was largely restored in 1872. The square Norman font of 12th century has elaborate decoration on all four sides. Registers date from 1538.

ST. MARY THE VIRGIN - LITTLE LAVER
CHARLES GRIGG TAIT

Loughton – St. Nicholas: Leave the High Street along the A121 going north towards Epping. At the foot of the hill a road, Rectory Lane, turns right and the church stands on the right side of the road, A113, adjacent to Loughton Hall, now a College of Further Education. The present small building, inside a small churchyard, dates from 1877 and stands on the site of the old village church of Loughton. It contains some stained glass of circa 1500 and there are brasses of 1541, 1558, 1594 and 1637. Note the very Gothic shrine of 1860 in the churchyard.

Loughton – St. John The Baptist: From Woodford proceed north into Loughton High Road and then into Church Hill, turning right into Church Lane. The church stands on the left side of a very narrow road, inside a very large graveyard surrounded by a brick wall and iron railings and entered by a tall lych gate. The very neat graveyard leads into a cemetery and is surrounded by tall trees and shrubs. It is a rather large building in the Neo-Norman style built in 1846 of brick and enlarged in 1877. Registers date from 1673.

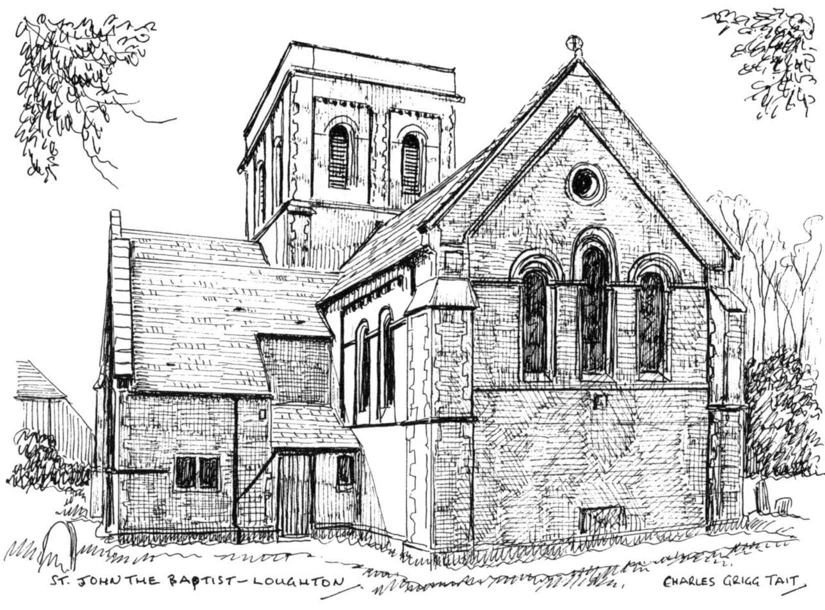

Loughton – St. Mary The Virgin: The church stands on the right side of the High Street going north on A121 on a slight hillock, inside a small rather crowded churchyard, surrounded by buildings on all sides. It is the local parish church to the town and is pure Victorian 1871-72.

ST. MARY MAGDALENE – MAGDALEN LAVER
CHARLES GRIGG TAIT

Magdalen Laver – St. Mary Magdalen: Take the turning left off the main road, going west from High Laver and proceed along a narrow gravel road, rather rough in places, to a cleared space. The church stands inside a small, well kept churchyard, entered through an iron fence via an iron kissing gate. The other side of the churchyard is bordered by a hedge. The building is of Norman origin with Roman brickwork, with 14th century additions and a small wooden bell tower of 15th century. There is a 14th century rood screen and the octagonal font is 15th century Perpendicular with some decoration. The whole building was restored in 1875. Registers date from 1557.

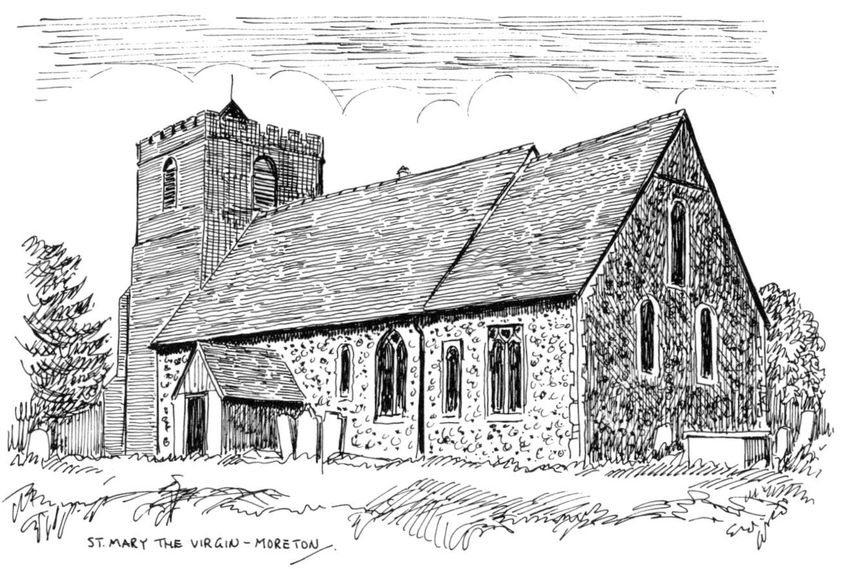

Moreton – St. Mary The Virgin: The church stands high up on a mound open to the road, inside a large well kept churchyard with several trees and bordered on three sides by a hedge. The entrance to the church is up a steep slope bordered by yew trees. The building consists of a 13th century nave and chancel with a later embattled west tower of 1787. Probably of Norman origin the church was largely restored in 1868-9. The square Norman font of Purbeck marble of the 12th century has decorated sides. Registers date from 1558.

Navestock – St. Thomas The Apostle: Going south from Chipping Ongar along the A113 turn left at the sign Navestock and the church stands left on a little side road. Inside a large churchyard surrounded by a low hedge it is entered through a very tall lych gate. The chancel end is rather obscured by a number of trees and shrubs. The building is of Norman origin, of stone with a timber tower and timber porch. It was restored in 1897 but was struck by a land mine in 1940 and then again, repaired. There are monuments to the Waldegrave family and several monuments from the 16th, 17th and 18th centuries. Registers date from 1538.

ST. THOMAS THE APOSTLE - NAVESTOCK
CHARLES GRIGG TAIT

North Weald Bassett – St. Andrew: Leave Epping north along the A1161 towards Chipping Ongar. At the junction with the A122 turn left and then left again down Vicarage Lane. The church stands on the right side of the road behind a row of cottages and the church hall, inside a fairly large churchyard entered through a large timber lych gate. There are some trees and shrubs surrounding the churchyard. Vicarage Lane is one way and exit is by way of a narrow road opposite the church on the left into the A1161, Wellington Road. The church is of Early English origin and built of flint and rubble of mainly 14th century with a 16th century embattled brick tower and six bells. It has been largely restored in 1867, 1885 and 1889. There is an old inscribed rood screen of 17th century and some 14th century stained glass. A brass is to Walter Lardner, wife and children 1606. Registers date from 1557.

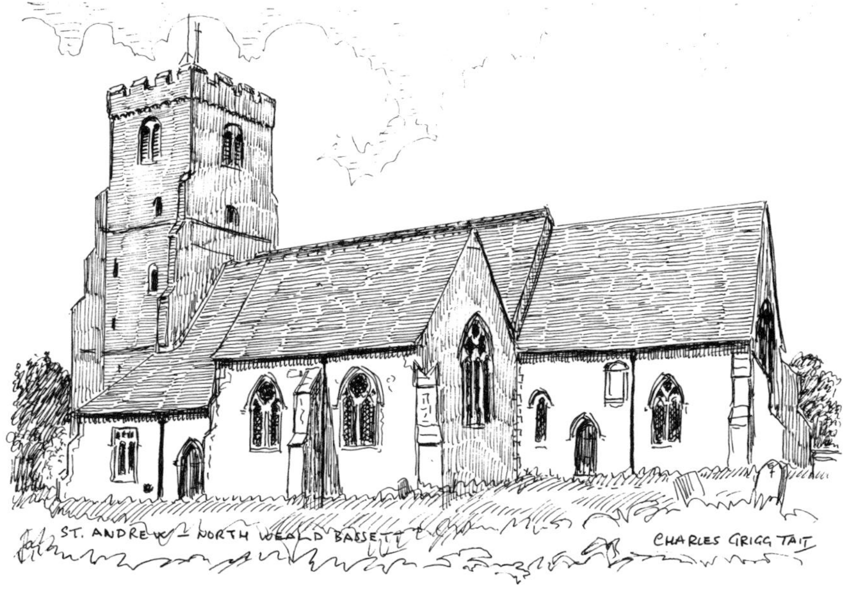

Norton Mandeville – All Saints: Turn left off the A122 towards Chelmsford at Norton Heath, then left again immediately after Norton Manor House, along a narrow road for about a mile to end in a cul-de-sac. The church stands in a small churchyard, adjacent to the Hall and entered by a wooden gateway and a stile. Apart from the farm buildings it is a very remote little church. The building is of Norman origin, consisting of nave and chancel of the 14th century, with a 15th century wooden belfry. The rood screen is 15th century and the square Norman font is late 12th century. The carved oak pulpit is 18th century. Registers date from 1538.

Shelley – St. Peter: Leave the B184 from Chipping Ongar to Fyfield at the sign 'Shelley Church' on the left side of the road. Follow a narrow road about half a mile to a cleared space. The church stands inside a fairly large churchyard, surrounded by tall trees and approached through a wooden fence by double gates. The whole building was rebuilt in 1811 and 1888, with a north west tower and spire. There is a brass to John Green 1626. Registers date from 1687.

Stapleford Abbotts – St. Mary: Proceed north from Havering-atte-Bower along the B175, passing through the village and turn sharp right at the Church sign into a very narrow winding lane. The church stands on a slight hillock inside a fairly large open churchyard entered by wooden gates on the south side and by steep steps at the tower end. There are several buildings surrounding the church. It is a small building largely rebuilt in 1862 with the yellow brick tower added in 1815. There is some early stained glass and a carved oak pulpit and some mural tablets to the Abdy family. Registers date from 1653.

Stapleford Tawney – St. Mary: Turn off right from the A113 from Chipping Ongar along a narrow winding road for about one mile. The church stands on the left side of the road inside a medium sized churchyard, rather overgrown and entered by a wooden gate. A number of trees line the entrance to the church. Of Early English origin it is a 13th century building of flint with a 15th century belfry and two bells. It was restored in 1861 and possesses a 19th century font.

Stanford Rivers – St. Margaret: Turn right off the A113 going south from Chipping Ongar and the church stands inside a large churchyard, surrounded by iron railings, close to the cross roads and adjacent to a large farm with many buildings. There are many graves and the churchyard is rather uneven in places. The church is stone built of Norman origin with later additions of the 13th and 14th centuries. The wooden belfry and spire, with two bells, is 15th century. There are brasses to Thomas Grevil 1492, Robert Barrow 1503, man and wife 1540 and Ann Napper and six sons 1584. The octagonal font is of Barnack stone circa 1200. Registers date from 1558.

ST. PETER AND ST. PAUL – STONDON MASSEY
CHARLES GRIGG TAIT

Stondon Massey – St. Peter And St. Paul: Follow the road as signposted through the village towards Chipping Ongar and the church is on the left side of a side road leading off right, inside a fairly large churchyard surrounded by a low fence and hedge. There are several tall trees and many gravestones. A gravel path leads from the wooden gates to the very fine timber porch. The building is of Norman origin with a timber belfry and spire. It was rebuilt in 1888, but with some original windows and doorways retrieved. There are brasses to John Sarre, 1570 and Rainold Hollingsworth and wife 1573. The octagonal font is 1400. Registers date from 1708.

Theydon Bois – St. Mary: Proceed from Abridge along the B172 into the village and turn off right at the road marked PIERCING HILL. The church stands immediately on the left, inside a medium sized churchyard and entered by a gravel path leading to the car park. Many trees and shrubs tend to obscure the church especially on the south side. The church is of brick and stone with a tower with three bells and was erected in 1850 on the site of a previous building. Registers date from 1717.

Theydon Garnon – All Saints (Coopersale): Proceed along a narrow lane to a sign marked COOPERSALE and HOBBS CROSS. The church stands on the left inside a large churchyard behind a wooden fence and entered by wooden gates. There are many tall trees near the tower end. The church is a stone building with a square embattled brick tower and five bells, with a timber south porch. It has been restored and enlarged. There is some 13th century and 15th century work in the main building. There are brasses to William Kirkaby, priest 1458 and to Elleyne Braunche, 1567 and monuments of the 17th and 18th centuries. A chest dated 1668 contains old documents and was presented by Sir John Archer, 1681. Registers date from 1558.

Theydon Mount – St. Michael The Archangel: Leave the A113 from Chipping Ongar, turning right at the sign 'The Theydons' along a narrow road and the church is on the left inside a fairly large open churchyard, on a slight mound. The churchyard is entered by wooden gates inside iron railings. There are a few trees and quite a large car park. The church is a small building of red brick with an embattled tower also of brick and rebuilt in 1600. There are many monuments to the Smyth family in a small chancel, the principal one to Sir Thomas Smyth 1577. The font is 17th century. Registers date from 1564.

Barstable Hundred

Basildon – Holy Cross: Leave the A127 from Southend at the entrance to Basildon A132 and turn right into Crane's Farm road, A1235. Turn sharp left at the roundabout by the Tractor Plant into a cul-de-sac leading into Crane's Court Housing Estate. A short walk leads directly to the church which stands inside a large, open, rather uneven graveyard surrounded by hedges. The church is now clear of the elm trees that previously surrounded it. The building is of brick and stone, mainly 15th century, but restored in 1880. The nave and chancel were rebuilt of brick in 1597 and the west tower has no buttresses. The south porch is a good example of 15th century timber work.

Billericay – St. Mary Magdalene: In the centre of the main street, the church stands on a corner at the junction of two road, on the site of a charity chapel. The building is of brick of 1780, but the embattled west tower, also of brick, is of Tudor origin with one bell. The clock commemorates Queen Victoria's Diamond Jubilee. The font is 18th century. Registers date from 1844.

Bowers Gifford – St. Margaret: Leave the B1464, old Pitsea to Southend road, turning right at a cul-de-sac sign, and then along a very narrow and uneven lane. The church stands on the left just before the railway bridge inside a small churchyard. Originally entered by a lych gate, it is now quite open and alongside the railway line. It is a small stone church of the 15th century with a western tower and spire with two 14th century bells. The octagonal font is Perpendicular 1500 and there is a brass to Sir John Gifford 1348. Registers date from 1558.

Brentwood – St. Thomas The Martyr: Turn off right from Ingrave Road into Hambro Road, almost opposite Brentwood School chapel and the church stands tall and impressive inside a small churchyard surrounded by a low hedge and some tall trees. The building itself dates from 1835. There are the remains of the old church in the High Street, 1221, dedicated to St. Thomas of Canterbury. The church has some relics of the old church in the shape of fragments of stained glass. It was enlarged in 1882 - 90. The tall tower and steeple are particularly noticeable. Registers date from 1695.

Bulphan – St. Mary: After turning left off the A127 at Dunton Wayletts take the B1007 going south towards Stanford Le Hope and turn right at the signpost 'Bulphan'. After crossing the A128, the church stands on the left inside a medium sized churchyard, entered through a lych gate set in a stone wall. The churchyard is fairly open with few trees and is surrounded by hedges. The church is a small stone building of the 14th century with a fine timber belfry and one bell. The south porch is of timber circa 1500 and there is an original chancel screen of the 15th century. Registers date from 1723.

THE HERITAGE CENTRE - FORMERLY ST. KATHERINE'S - CANVEY ISLAND
CHARLES GRIGG TAIT

Canvey Island – St. Katherine: The church, now renamed the 'St. Katherine in the Village Heritage Centre', stands on the left side of the main road to the village, Canvey Road, inside a large churchyard entered through a wooden lych gate. It is a small wooden building first erected in 1662, but subsequently rebuilt many times. The present building is 1875 and has a turret with one bell. Registers date from 1819.

Chadwell St. Mary – St. Mary: Leave the A127 from Southend at the Halfway House and proceed south along the A128 to the junction with the Linford Road and the church stands on the corner on the right side of the road inside a small open churchyard. The church is largely Norman, but very much restored. Most of the present building is 14th and 15th century. The west tower is circa 1500 and the north and south doorways are distinctly Norman. Registers date from 1539.

ST. MARY - CHADWELL ST. MARY
CHARLES GRIGG TAIT

Corringham – St. Mary: Leave Fobbing church turning left into Fobbing road and left again when entering Church Lane. The church stands on the right side of the road opposite the Bull public house in a small churchyard entered by wooden gates through a low stone wall. Some trees obscure the north side. Of early Norman origin the church is a flint and stone building of mainly 13th century, but with a distinctive Norman west tower with a pyramid roof. The chantry chapel is enclosed by a carved oak screen. There are brasses to Alice George 1453, Richard de Beltoun 1340, a civilian 1460 and Thomas at-Lee 1467. The octagonal font is 13th century. Registers date from 1558.

Doddinghurst – All Saints: Turn right off the B1002, the old road to Brentwood into the village and the church stands on the right side of the road opposite the village hall. Inside a large rather rambling churchyard, surrounded by a tall wooden fence, it is entered from the road side through a low hedge by wooden gates. Of Early English origin the building consists of various periods from the 13th to the 16th centuries and it was restored in 1853. The timber belfry is 16th century and the timber south porch is one of the finest in the county. The octagonal font is 14th century. Registers date from 1559.

Downham – St. Margaret: From Ramsden Heath proceed east towards Downham and take the right fork south towards Wickford. The church stands on the left side of the road, inside a large churchyard entered by a lych gate and surrounded by hedges. By the church entrance is an old building, part of the church property and is an 18th century dovecote. The church was rebuilt in 1871 except for the 15th century brick tower and timber south porch. It was extensively damaged recently by arson, but is now restored. There are various monuments of the 18th and 19th centuries under the tower. Registers date from 1558.

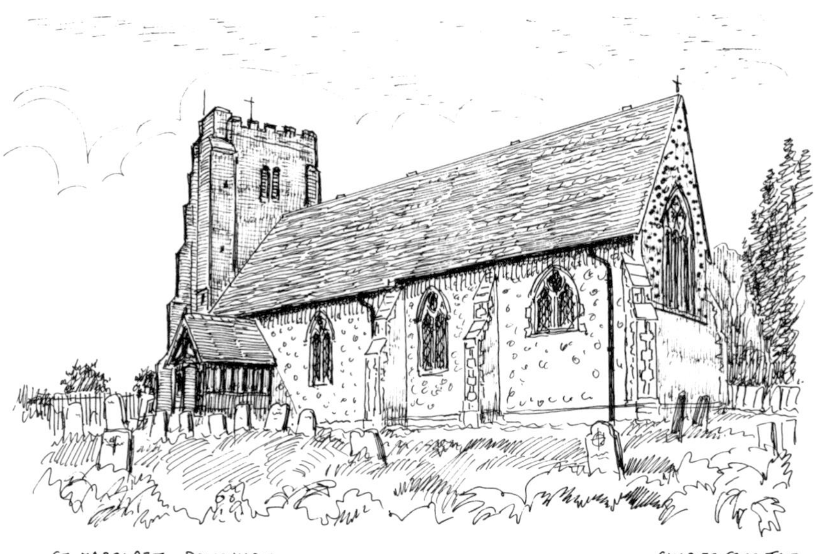

Dunton – St. Mary: Leave the A127 from Southend at Dunton Wayletts, turning left into the B1007. The church is situated at the end of a right turning into a narrow road. It is now a private residence and entry is no longer possible. The original 16th century church stood on the site of a previous 12th century priory used as a resting place for the pilgrims on the way to Canterbury, until destroyed. It was then rebuilt in 1873 of red brick with a timber tower and one bell. Some of the timbers of the old church were preserved. Registers date from 1538.

East Horndon – All Saints: The church stands high up on a hill overlooking the London Southend arterial road A127 where it joins the A128 and close to the Halfway House Inn. Now disused the building stands alone in a cleared and well kept churchyard, remote except for a small barn which stands to the north of the church. It is a low squat building of red Tudor brick, restored in 1908 and again in the 1970's, with a tower of brick with four bells. Inside the Tyrell chapel are monuments to Alice, Lady Tyrell and ten children 1422, Sir Thomas Tyrell 1476 and Sir John Tyrell 1766. The square font is Norman circa 1200. Registers date from 1558.

East Tilbury – St. Catherine: Leave Stanford-le-Hope proceeding south from the A1013, through Linford towards Coalhouse Fort. The church, on the left, stands on a little hillock inside a fairly large grassy churchyard, entered through iron gates. The road here is very narrow. Of Norman-Transitional origin it is mainly an Early English building. Some damage was sustained from the Dutch fleet in 1667 according to local tradition. There is a table tomb to John Rawlinse 1698 and to Sir Henry Knight 1721 and a brass to William de Bordfield. The octagonal font is 16th century. Registers date from 1627.

Fobbing – St. Michael The Archangel: Situated on the left side of the road leaving the A13 roundabout to the south and marked Fobbing High Road. The church is inside a large churchyard behind a stone wall entered through two sets of iron gates. Some tall trees obscure the south side. Of Anglo-Saxon origin, but mainly 14th and 15th century, it is a tall stone building with an embattled west tower with five bells, mainly 15th century. There is a fine timber south porch of 15th century. A general restoration took place in 1905-6. A Purbeck marble monument in Norman French, 14th century, asks prayers for Thomas de Crawdene. The octagonal font of Purbeck marble is 13th century. Registers date from 1539.

Great Burstead – St. Mary Magdalen: Leaving Billericay by the A176 proceed south, taking the left turn marked Great Burstead. The church stands on the right side of the road behind a low brick wall inside a large churchyard which slopes rather steeply to the south side. Of Norman origin and on the site of an earlier Saxon church, it is mainly 14th and 15th century with a 14th century stone tower and spire. The church was enlarged in the 14th and 15th centuries. There are two medieval oak porches, about 15th century or later. The plain octagonal font is 15th century. There is a monument to James Fishpoole 1767. Registers date from 1558.

ST. MARY MAGDALEN – GREAT BURSTEAD
CHARLES GRIGG TAIT

Horndon-on-the-Hill – St. Peter And St. Paul: Leave the A13 from Basildon, turning right along the B1007. In about one mile, a sharp turning left, signposted Horndon-On-The-Hill leads back into the village. The church is situated inside a small churchyard behind some houses along a narrow lane and is entered by a lych gate. The south side is partly obscured by trees. Of Early English origin the church is mainly 13th century with a 15th century chancel and timber tower on a very spectacular wooden frame. There is a monument to David Caldwell and wife 1634. The square decorated font is a very good example of 14th century work. Registers date from 1672.

ST. PETER AND ST. PAUL – HORNDON-ON-THE-HILL
CHARLES GRIGG TAIT

Hutton – All Saints: Proceed along the A129 towards Billericay turning right at the sign CHURCH on to a narrow road with traffic calming humps. At the far end turn left into Church Lane and the church stands on the right inside a fairly large churchyard behind a wooden fence, entered by double wooden gates. It is a small stone building with a 15th century timber turret and five bells. Rebuilt in 1873, at least some 14th century work of the medieval church remains. There is a brass to a man and wife and sixteen children, 1520. Registers date from 1654.

Ingrave – St. Nicholas: The church stands on the left side of the road from Brentwood A128, almost opposite the village post office, inside a large very crowded churchyard. It is entered first by a lych gate and then iron gates through iron railing Many trees line the approach to the entrance which is in the tower. The church is a large red brick building erected by Robert Lord Petre in 1735 to replace the old parish churches of West Horndon and Ingrave. There are brasses to Margaret Fitz-Lewis 1450, to John Fitz-Lewis and four wives 1500 and to Margaret Wake 1466. The octagonal font is 15th century. Registers date from 1560.

Laindon – St. Nicholas: The church stands in a commanding position on a hill top on a side road leading off the centre of the town. The medium sized churchyard is approached by steep steps and is rather uneven in places. It is a small stone building of mainly 13th century, with a timber belfry and spire. There is a two storied priest house at the west end, 15th century, which was restored in 1881. The timber south porch is 14th century. There are two brasses 1480 and 1510 to two priests. The square Purbeck marble font is 13th century. Registers date from 1636.

ST. MARY THE VIRGIN AND ALL SAINTS – LANGDON HILLS
CHARLES GRIGG TAIT

Langdon Hills (Old) – St. Mary The Virgin And All Saints: Leave the A127 from Southend at Dunton Wayletts, turning left into the B1007 and then left again into a narrow lane signposted 'Unfit for motors'. Proceeding up hill the church stands on the left, inside a large churchyard surrounded by a brick wall. It is now a private house. The original building was of 16th century brick work, with a north chapel added about 1621. The timber belfry was rebuilt in 1842. There is a royal coat of arms dated 1660. Registers date from 1686.

ST. MARY THE VIRGIN AND ALL SAINTS – LANGDON HILLS
CIRCA 1950.

Langdon Hills (New) – St. Mary: Climb the very steep Crown Hill up from Laindon and the church stands on the right side of the road opposite a house with iron gates. It is a tall narrow building of Kentish ragstone, 1877, and stands on the edge of a steep slope so that there is no churchyard possible.

Little Burstead – St. Mary: Going south from Billericay along the A176 take the right fork at Laindon Common past Stockwell Hall. The church is at the end of a gravel path, to the right of the road inside a large, very uneven churchyard, entered through a wooden gate. It stands high on a small hill, surrounded by a tall hedge and trees. A small 13th century building of puddingstone it has a turret and two bells of the 15th century. Some later additions of the 14th and 15th centuries are in the windows. There are some 18th century monuments and brasses and an octagonal font of the 15th century. Registers date from 1681.

Mucking – St. John Baptist: Leave Stanford-le-Hope turning left from the church and proceeding south towards East Tilbury. About one mile along turn left into a narrow road over the railway level crossing and the church stands on the left behind a stone wall inside a large churchyard. At the time of writing the church is in the process of becoming a private property. The church was rebuilt in 1887 from a ruinous condition, of stone and marble with an embattled west tower and three bells. Some of the earlier features have been retained. There is a monument to Elizabeth Downes 1608. Registers date from 1558.

Nevendon – St. Peter: Approaching Basildon from Wickford on the A132 and after passing under the A127 the new complex of the Sainsbury shopping centre is on the left and a sharp turning just past the centre enters Nevendon Road. Turn right into Church Lane by Nevendon Hall and the church stands inside a small churchyard. It is entered by a damaged lych gate and is surrounded by a brick wall on one side and houses on the other. A small 13th and 14th century stone church it was restored in 1875. Registers date from 1669.

North Benfleet – All Saints: Leave the B1464, Pitsea to Southend road at the left turning marked Pound Lane and proceed north before turning right into a narrow lane which becomes a very rough track ending in a group of farm buildings. The church stands inside a small very overgrown churchyard, entered by wooden gates and adjacent to a large pond, possibly the remains of the now demolished North Benfleet Hall moat. Of Norman origin it is a small stone building of the 13th century with a timber belfry and two bells, now covered by a brick tower of 1903. The church was restored in 1871, but is now at the time of writing, in a very dilapidated condition and much neglected. The square Purbeck marble font is 13th century. Registers date from 1647.

Orsett – St. Giles And All Saints: Leave the A127 from Southend at the Halfway House and proceed south on the A128, turning off right at the sign Orsett into the village, about one mile. The church stands inside a large churchyard opposite a row of picturesque buildings, fronted by a stone wall and entered by wooden gates. Some trees block the view in the front of the church and the graveyard is rather uneven in places. The church is a flint and stone building of Norman origin, but with some restoration in 1894. It is of unusual plan and has a tower built partly of stone and 17th century brick. The south doorway is Norman and of particular interest. There is an octagonal font with some decoration of 1500 Perpendicular style. There are brasses to Thomas Latham, wife and children 1485, to Robert Kinge 1584 and a civilian 1535 and there are many wall monuments. Registers date from 1669.

Pitsea – St. Michael: The church stands traditionally high up overlooking the marshes and railway station inside a rather crowded churchyard. At the time of writing the building is now cut off by the new A130 (A13) road and has suffered some dereliction. It is a small stone building of Perpendicular style 1400 - 1500, but was rebuilt in 1871 except for the embattled west tower. Registers date from 1688.

Ramsden Bellhouse – St. Mary: Leave the A129 at the foot of Crays Hill, turning left towards Ramsden Heath. The church stands on the left side of the road inside a large, cleared churchyard, open to the road and surrounded by low hedges. Of Perpendicular origin it is a stone building with timber tower and spire, largely rebuilt in 1880. The south porch and belfry are 14th and 15th century and the octagonal font is 15th century. Registers date from 1667.

Ramsden Crays – St. Mary: Turn sharp left nearly at the top of Crays Hill on the A129 and proceed along a narrow very rough lane for about one mile and the church stands at the end. Inside a fairly large churchyard enclosed by iron railings it is entered by two sets of iron gates. It is a very remote little building and was much restored in 1870 - 71. There are some 15th century remains in the windows and a timber belfry. Registers date from 1558.

Shenfield – St. Mary The Virgin: Turn off the main road to Brentwood A1023 at the sign 'Shenfield Parish Church' along a narrow winding road and the church is on the left hand side after a double bend. It is situated inside a fairly crowded churchyard with many trees and enclosed by a hedge and is entered by a wooden lych gate and a side gate. The church is of Early English origin but mainly 13th century with additions in the 15th century. The tall timber west tower and spire with five bells are also 15th century. The building was restored and enlarged in 1840, 1863, 1868 and 1887. There is a marble table tomb to Elizabeth Robinson 1652. The font is octagonal Perpendicular circa 1390. Registers date from 1539.

South Benfleet – St. Mary: The church is situated on the corner of the High Street, opposite the Anchor public house before turning right towards the railway station and Canvey Island. The churchyard is surrounded by a brick capped stone wall and entered by a lych gate and two open entrances. A number of tall trees tend to obscure the building. Of Norman origin, the church is a large stone building of mainly 15th century, but very much restored. The large embattled west tower with spire is of 14th century origin. Of particular interest is the exceptionally fine timber south porch circa 1450. Registers date from 1573.

ST. MARGARET OF ANTIOCH– STANFORD-LE-HOPE
CHARLES GRIGG TAIT

Stanford-le-hope – St. Margaret Of Antioch: Situated in the centre of the town on a corner, the church is inside a large churchyard entered through a lych gate and surrounded by a stone wall. Many trees obscure the south side. There is a large church car park. The building is of Norman origin with additions in 13th and 14th centuries. The tower with six bells is 15th century, but was rebuilt in 1877. The whole church was also restored and hides much of the original building. It is rather a large impressive church. There is a doorway to a rood staircase and a screen at the west end of the chapel. There is a table tomb 1500 and a monument to Sir Heneage Fetherstone 1711. The font is 13th century Purbeck marble. Registers date from 1680.

Thundersley – St. Peter: The church is visible from quite a distance as it stands high up on a hill. Leave the Tarpots corner on the B1464 and before ascending Bread and Cheese Hill turn left along Rhoda Road North and then right up into Church Road. The church stands at the top, inside a very large churchyard, entered by a wooden lych gate. Most of the gravestones lie to the east of the church as it slopes down to the road. It is a stone building of Norman origin, but restored in 1885, with a timber tower and spire and two bells of the 15th century. There are 13th century additions, but the main alteration is the large extension to the nave and chancel end. The octagonal font is 14th century Perpendicular with decorated faces. Registers date from 1569.

Vange – All Saints: Situated high up on a hill almost opposite the school on the left side of the B1464 from Pitsea. The large churchyard to the north is very crowded and the church is approached by a long gravel path. Of Norman origin it is a small building of stone and rubble of mainly 15th century. The small timber bell tower is 1761 and there is some old stained glass in the east window. The church was restored in 1837. The square font is transitional 12th century There are monuments to George Moule 1669 and Mary 1659 with a royal coat of arms William III 1687. Registers date from 1558.

West Tilbury – St. James: Leave East Tilbury going north again and fork left at the sign West Tilbury. The church is situated on the left behind a small green, inside a fairly large churchyard, rather overgrown, and entered through a lych gate. At the time of writing the building was in the process of being renovated. The church is a stone building of the 13th century with later additions and the embattled west tower was erected in 1883. Registers date from 1540.

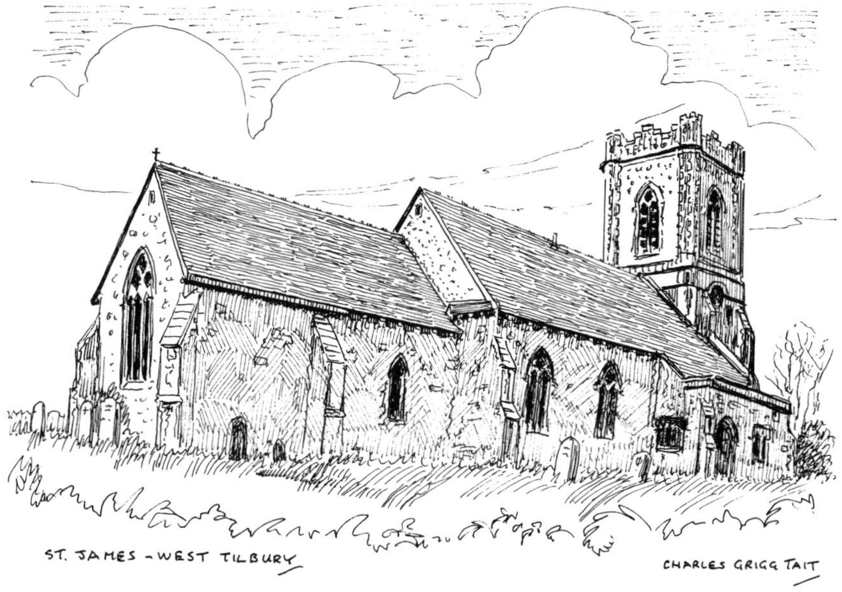

Wickford – St. Catherine: Approach Wickford from Rayleigh on the A129 and the church stands on the right side of the road inside a medium sized graveyard which is entered by a wooden gate. The churchyard is rather overcrowded and uneven in places. The church is a stone building with a west tower with two bells. It was rebuilt in 1876 in the Early English style, but retains some of the old 14th century roof timbers. The octagonal font is 15th century. There is a stone slab to the Rev. Thomas Case and wife Sarah 1730-1761. Registers date from 1538.